Gathering Petals

REBECCA JOY

BookLeaf Publishing

India | USA | UK

Presentation by *BookLeaf Publishing*

Web: www.bookleafpub.com

E-mail: info@bookleafpub.com

ISBN: 9789360941086

First edition 2024

DEDICATION

for PH and ND,

this is for every time you've said 'don't worry' and then proceeded to worry yourself.

ACKNOWLEDGEMENTS

I extend my heartfelt gratitude to the incredible people who have played a crucial role in the journey of writing this small collection.

To my friends, thank you for being there to read and re-read, offering criticism but more support than I ever imagined. Your encouragement, late-night conversations and shared moments of creativity have fuelled my poems. A lot of you have acted as inspiration for these pieces. It's your lives and stories that have broadened my perspective and the way I look at life.

In particular, I'm grateful to IHH for your absolutely genius poems and free words of advice.

To my teachers, your guidance and mentorship have been invaluable.

Thank you for caring enough to look for opportunities and pushing me to do them.

I am also thankful to my family for their unwavering support, understanding and encouragement.

This little book of emotions has been a collaborative effort, and I deeply appreciate everyone who has contributed to it.

With sincere gratitude,

Rebecca

PREFACE

Hey there!

This little book is for young people like me.

Here, you essentially discover that you're not alone in all the emotions you've faced and are facing; you are human after all.

The way I intended for you to read this is a method of mindlessness while actually being mindful in the process.

Whenever you're feeling low or just don't have anything to do, open up a random page, start reading and forget your problems for a little while.

If you want to read through it in one go, that's up to you.

Or if you're like me, skip the preface altogether.

I hope you like what you read, and of course, you're meant to judge and interpret it any way you like; that's the whole point of poetry.

Women

Some women are made of stars,
that illuminate when you see no hope,
others are made of wars,
that fight your battles when you can no more.

some are made of music and song,
to be with you, when all you can hear is the
humming of your heart,
and others are made of scars,
bearing unhealing wounds, housing your pain.

if you ask me what woman I am,
I can't say,
for I am no woman yet,
but the one I want to become is one like the sea,
where you'll find serenity.

The text game

He's left you on read
when really, he saw your message but is
attending tuitions,
he said ok?
was that passive-aggressive?
was it meant to block your airway?
he replied with a thumbs up,
was he mad?
did he care to stay?
he didn't even see the message, but you're
already thinking of possible ways to explain
why he's taking so long,
does he hate you?
does he know something he won't say?

To Read between the lines

When you see me cry
please (don't) walk away
and know that there's nothing you can do (but
stay)
and don't open your mouth (except to tell me
how much you care)
and don't hold my hand (unless you don't mind it
when people stare)

C'est la vie

sometimes in life
you have to compromise, they say
you need to give her the benefit of the doubt
you need to just stay

and stick around while she treats you
like a piece of gum under her shoe
you have to let it go, they say
say it's all good with you

sometimes in life,
you have to learn to understand
that no matter what you do, she'll take it the
wrong way
and accept that there's nothing you can do but
stay

they say she's just like that,
bound to make mistakes,
bound to often outrage
bound to spit in your face

with words, no person should hear,
she's the one to be feared

Uncertainties

When it's the end of the world
and there's nothing to see
would you still come searching for me

would you cross the ocean,
blindfold on your eyes
just to hear my voice,
to hear my adieu one last time

when your hope runs out
would you survive on mine and,
crawl through the desert
just to be with me as you cry

about all the times you thought you had left to
say the things you never did
I would sigh

when you know that it's over,
would you still say a prayer
to meet me again sometime, somewhere?

Birthdays

Every year you're expected to grow older
I mean, universal fact.
but why does my mind now know way more
than it's supposed to
while my heart stays right there, the same as
when I was two,
the same sense of justice.
why have my soul's instincts grown stronger
how can I pick lies apart?
so much has changed,
but I still feel
like unfinished art

Letting go...

It's always difficult,
when you know you deserve better
but didn't get what you need
just when you think you've seen pain
it comes crashing down like you couldn't
explain,

what was happening,
too much, too soon,
too late to process
too difficult to understand.

when you forget what really matters
and this becomes your all,
it's okay–
they say,
it's okay.

it's not okay.

To give up on a person

Why bother?
she's going to take it the wrong way.
why re-check?
she's going to react no matter what you say.
why overthink it?
you can't do anything but stay,
and listen to her complain about the negatives,
context in the grey.
why pick yourself apart?
when you know she thinks you don't have a
heart.
why care at all?
when you've done what you could for her, but
conveniently, that she refuses to recall.

Gratitude

I'm grateful for the people who've taught me
how to live,
how to be in the moment
without wondering what's to come.

and I'm grateful for the people who've shown me
what love is,
how to love, how to accept
without denying I deserve

for the people who've made me laugh,
who've been there in the darkest times
to charge the torch with a smile.

Colours

Blue like the sky filled with innocent beasts
red like the fire in her eyes, so deep
yellow like the stars, sparkling with hope
and green like the hills, those gentle slopes.

orange like the goldfish, the happiest in,
the indigo water, home, the sea
pink like the rose, a symbol of love,
also the colour of the heart, the trove

black like the yin, filled with pain,
but white like the yang, whose peace it needn't
feign.

For George

When he's looked at
his image speaks volumes but then barely
whispers

his heart tells the story of a person who loved
so deeply, you couldn't even begin to fathom
how that love ran
like blood in his veins
only to be then,
pierced by a needle to numb the pain.
now his heart lay cold, not daring to beat, for it
would wake the hopeless, beaten beast.

(her) circle of life

I saw her on that stretcher,
still and beaten,
covered in burns and scarlet
eyes closed, life in completion.

brought in at 10:50,
declared doa,

cause of death, gas explosion.

she was a girl who didn't dare dream
for she knew with that dash of vermillion,
that she was just a vessel,
to serve and be abused.
hurt.
dented.

I saw her body being wheeled out of the
operation theatre,
her baby girl distraught,
as if she somehow knew that she was the reason,
her mother was gone.

Oh Juliet!

It is my lady; it is my love,
my heart broke in two when I heard those words,
for in star-crossed love stories like ours
hope doesn't come in herds

his words plunged like a dagger,
Romeo and I would be apart,
for all eternity, our loss,
all for two egoistic hearts.

Pearls and poppies

She knew it was to come,
her time with pearls and poppies,
her existence would someday cease,
but was it too much to wait?

she thought, maybe it's worth it?
maybe life would make sense in a month?
but as the calendar flipped by,
all she felt was closer to her pearls and poppies.

all it took was a trip to the pharmacy,
she needed the morphine, for many weeks,
for she wouldn't come back,
and so the bulk payment was done.

maybe she figured it would all go away,
her mind would stop going to that place,
where oysters die and poppies dry,
but it would never happen,
so she was gone,
to the pills that were her pearls,
To the thoughts that were her poppies.

Music

It's everywhere you go,
everything you hear
is music to a certain someone's ear

it's in the trees, with the woodpecker's rhythm,
in the breeze as the brook babbles on
in the gaze of the amazed toddler
as she learns a rhyme
in the pond, as the toad croaks in time.

in your heart with every beat,
in your fingers, as you try to resist the urge to
drum on the seat,
in your voice, if you just let go.

Priorities

When time feels like a self-absorbing mess,
and your mind has serious trouble with distress,
wondering what's more important,
while it drifts to daunting possibilities and to the
grace period, ignorant.

for when time has been given,
procrastination works its magic.
causing half the time to go into supposed
'preparation',
and the other into overthought feelings of regret,
classic.

Reality checks

The next time you feel things are all going south
take a step back,
and look for the grout,

the tiny spaces in life that haven't been filled will
always seem like the end of the world
until you realise slowly,
that the grout's holding it firm

so no matter what falls out of place,
it's all a matter of some cement and water,
to fill the gaps, to fill your space.

Happiness 101

I used to think there was a secret to happiness
something I hadn't discovered,
turns out I was right
though the truth was merely discoloured

you see, it's not supposed to come in waves
like it once did, when every event was a
distraction,
from my thoughts and where they led me,
from the dissatisfaction

with myself,
with where I was in life,
with the people I was with,
but you know, change is inevitable, so change it
did

the process is obscured most times
with constant pain till you feel no more
but unless you help yourself, there's no way
you'll get there
so here's how to spare yourself the gore

there's a simple formula,
and it'll eventually make sense

expect of others what they expect of you
for a lot of our happiness comes from validation,
I know, not a major sensation
but trust the process, and everything works out
for the best,
and how you'll get there?
that's the rest.

the impossible dream

the winds blow away from the slightest touch
the things one needs to survive (or dreams of as
much)
with every sprint,
every wish the star recounts,
the dream drifts further, out of touch

from hand to hand, the wish passes on,
the people who dream can't work upon
so instead they wish upon an eyelash, lone
waiting for the dream to magically unfold

work hard, they won't,
but rely on the universe
unknowing of the fact that without effort,
their dreams are merely words

so they sit and complain and ask and blame,
the poor black cat who was just on his way
obliviating the reason their dreams don't come
true,
but stay wishes, as the stars slowly grew.

Oh lady, my lady.

oh lady
where do you go
would you be mine
or would you rather lie low

oh lady, so pretty
why do you cry
when I merely ask you
if you'll be mine?

oh young lady
oh how you run,
with the body of your scarf around your neck
but the tip, grasped by my thumbs

oh lovely lady
why can't you stay?
just because I touch your face,
doesn't mean you should go away.

oh sly female!
why do you scream?
why be such a tease?
I stop you on your way back home,
and no one's here to see,

but still, you cannot come with,
trusting the unknown stranger, me?

22

If The Walls Could Talk

Where is my child?
Where is she?
The hasty gestures made of her hands
The mother's eyes, bloodshot and dilated,
Large eyes, the pain all the more seen.
Her movement, aimless but rushed,
Hands now folded together, pleading with the
nurse,
To see her baby, the child that was of her.
I heard a heart-wrenching cry and saw her
mourn,
as she stared at the child, hers, stillborn.

Change

So change, she said,
Lose your accent, lose your touch
lose your small nose, lose the full lips,
lose the grace you possess,
Lose your feet, arched by the pointe shoes,
lose your hands that express what your words
can't,
Lose your perfect eyebrows, they'll only lead to
wrinkles,
lose your caramel eyes, it's a maze you'll get lost
in,
Lose your heart, open and caring,
lose your body, flexible to the core,
Lose your hips, they're just used to distract, no?
lose the very essence of you,
let it be gone to the whims of the wind,
and then look at what you possess.
'Well then I'd have nothing', I said
so look at what you want now; is it not to
change?
so if your change led to this,
Wouldn't you be better off just staying the
same?
I said, 'you're one to speak'

she said, 'I'm telling you love, change I did, and
it is still what I seek'
25

Relationship Goals

26

Take of me what you have none of
I'll keep you safe when you cry
Hurt me and you'll still have me
If only I knew how to, from this cycle, untie

In Another World

27

If glass was opaque
I guess my eyes would be spared
Of half the nightmares they've seen
If mirrors didn't reflect
Maybe that'd help
With my image of me.

Village Female

She was oppressed, not given a voice,
As she sat there dainty and poised,
All she wanted was to speak,
Not just cook and clean and be,
A mother to her children three,
No, she was much more,
As she sat there dainty and poised,
She had the wits of a hundred men.

If only, she thought to herself,
They would treat her like a person and not just a
creature,
Born only to serve them.

She wanted, more than ever, to come up with a
way,
For women like her, from everywhere, to come
and speak their minds,
For their husbands, fathers and all village folk,
to listen to them opine;
On the problems that affected them,
The village's unsung pillars,
And not just some hearsay on politicians who
there don't,

give their wives or sisters or daughters any
freedom of thought,
It's gone on so far that even they wonder if they
deserve.

Even she, at twenty, wanted a life,
Not restricted to the walls of 'her' house,
She wanted to govern
But was silenced time and again.

They told her to find peace in that monotony.

She gave up on herself but stood by her
daughter,
Through failures and pain,
And not one day did she find peace,
Not one day had she taken any rest,
That is, until the day she passed,
There she found eternal peace,
For her daughter had been elected chief.
So she lay there, dainty and poised,
Not breathing, not tense,
But those who saw her knew,
There was a girl whose dreams she stood by,
A revolution she helped commence.

Endless Cycles

He was a product of his pain.
Every action he did that didn't suit the occasion
was immediately attributed to his past.
He was a shadow of his past.
Every word he spoke that tried to empathise,
Only reminded him of his story.
Every look he took into the world outside
reflected in his eyes as nothing but tragedy.
He chose his present to live in his past and never
saw a future.
He was a product of his pain,
Choosing to not let go, until he was but grain.